The Story of Codey Crowe

Karen Murphy

MAPLE
PUBLISHERS

The Story of Codey Crowe

Author: Karen Murphy

Copyright © Karen Murphy (2024)

The right of Karen Murphy to be identified as author of this work has been asserted by the author in accordance with section 77 and 78 of the Copyright, Designs and Patents Act 1988.

First Published in 2024

ISBN 978-1-83538-283-7 (Paperback)

Published by:
    Maple Publishers
    Fairbourne Drive, Atterbury,
    Milton Keynes,
    MK10 9RG, UK
    www.maplepublishers.com

A CIP catalogue record for this title is available from the British Library.

All rights reserved. No part of this book may be reproduced or translated by any form or by any means, electronic or mechanical, including photocopying, recording or by any information storage and retrieval system without written permission from the author.

The views expressed in this work are solely those of the author and do not necessarily reflect the views of the publisher, and the publisher hereby disclaims any responsibility for them.

This is the story of Codey Crowe,

He loves to bounce and he loves to throw.

He'll bounce on the trampoline,

high in the air.

He'll bounce on the bed,

the sofa, the chair.

He likes to throw objects and watch them fall.

Especially odd things not just a ball.

He throws things like pencils or pieces of wood,

Toy cars, tv controls.....spoons are good!

He likes things that spin,

he just loves to go round.

Then enjoys himself stimming,

especially with sound!

He likes to eat carrots and broccoli and swede.

Tomatoes and pasta, he likes a good feed!

He has so much energy he swings high and low.

He is sensory seeking, that much we know.

He climbs in the cupboard

and also the fridge.

He adores the climbing frame,

sits on the bridge.

He likes to go swimming

and loves to jump in.

Maybe one day The Olympics???? ...

..... and win!!!!

He loves watching the wind,

blowing the trees.

It's his favourite thing,

it puts him at ease.

The rain doesn't bother him,

he likes to get wet.

He'll stay out all day

until the sun starts to set.

He has two lovely sisters,

Darcey and Nell.

They play with him daily

and care for him well.

Codey's autistic,

he can't talk to us yet.

But he knows what he wants

and he knows how to get!

We are truly blessed with this wonderful boy.

He makes us so happy he's a bundle of joy.

Yes he is different

and it can get quite mad.

But all of the good things

outweigh the bad.

His smile and his laughter

will light up your day.

He has a place in this world

and he'll find his way!

www.ingramcontent.com/pod-product-compliance
Lightning Source LLC
Chambersburg PA
CBHW040023130526
44590CB00036B/69